Magical
Journey
Meditations

Magical Journey Meditations

Lisa Mastrocola

BALBOA.
PRESS

A DIVISION OF HAY HOUSE

Balboa Press books may be ordered through booksellers or by contacting:

Balboa Press
A Division of Hay House
1663 Liberty Drive
Bloomington, IN 47403
www.balboapress.com
1-(877) 407-4847

Because of the dynamic nature of the Internet, any web addresses or links contained in this book may have changed since publication and may no longer be valid. The views expressed in this work are solely those of the author and do not necessarily reflect the views of the publisher, and the publisher hereby disclaims any responsibility for them.

The author of this book does not dispense medical advice or prescribe the use of any technique as a form of treatment for physical, emotional, or medical problems without the advice of a physician, either directly or indirectly. The intent of the author is only to offer information of a general nature to help you in your quest for emotional and spiritual well-being. In the event you use any of the information in this book for yourself, which is your constitutional right, the author and the publisher assume no responsibility for your actions.

Certain stock imagery © Thinkstock.
Any people depicted in stock imagery provided by Thinkstock are models, and such images are being used for illustrative purposes only.

Printed in the United States of America

ISBN: 978-1-4525-6855-3 (e)
ISBN: 978-1-4525-6851-5 (sc)

Library of Congress Control Number: 2013902543

Balboa Press rev. date: 4/23/2013

Table of Contents

1. Meet Your Guardian Angel 1
2. Magic Carpet Ride 4
3. Fairyland 7
4. Magical Telescope 10
5. Wishing Well 13
6. Cloud Connection 16
7. Three, Two, One … Blast Off! 19
8. Santa's Sleigh 22
9. Go Fly a Kite! 25
10. The Magic Castle 28
11. The Lucky Leprechaun 31
12. The Traveling Suitcase 34
13. Unicorn Land 37
14. Fluttering Butterflies 40
15. The Bunny Trail 43
16. Boat Ride Ocean Side 46
17. Magic Slippers 49
18. All Aboard! 52
19. The Dream Box 55
20. Talkin' Dolphin 58
21. The Amazing Spectacles 61
22. On the Wings of a Dove 64

Thanks to Joe, Joseph, Jenna, Anthony,
Risa Grossman, and the Jamal family

Special thanks to all my "magical journey" students

Introduction

About six years ago, I began meditating on a regular basis. I found that afterward I felt more relaxed, and my concentration greatly improved. Through meditation, I was able to connect more deeply to spirit and the angels. The angels guided me to write this book because they felt it was very important for children to stay connected.

I have noticed that there are many self-help books for adults. As a first-grade teacher, I was always looking for ways to educate my students. When my students, as well as my own children, would tell me that they were having trouble sleeping or were feeling anxious about tests and meeting new people, I felt that teaching them to meditate would help them become grounded, focused, and relaxed. I started an after-school program called Magical Journey Kids. I wrote magical journey meditations and followed up each meditation with a sharing time and a craft. The class became very popular, and I received many requests to write these meditations in a book. I also used my meditations with my entire first-grade class before writing assignments, tests, or class parties. The students' parents could not believe how calm the children were right after a meditation.

The format of these meditations is based on my Magical Journey Kids after-school class:

- A simple breathing technique (see Roller Coaster Breathing Exercise)
- A guided meditation (approximately five minutes)
- Sharing time
- An art project or visual aid

Children have a unique way of looking at life. Just imagine the fun they will have when they take a magical journey wearing magical slippers, look through a magical telescope, or explore with magical glasses. What messages do the clouds hold? Who knows? The sky's the limit!

Parents

Think about the day you've had today. Was any part of it stressful? How did that make you feel? How do you feel when you enter a room full of people you don't know? How do you feel when you have a big day coming up, such as a big presentation or a big exam? How about when you have a stressful job or just lots of errands to run and not enough time? All these feelings of stress and anxiety have the same effect on a child. No wonder so many people have trouble sleeping.

As a society, we really don't take enough time to quiet our bodies or connect with spirit and the angels. God knew that life on earth could get stressful. Therefore, being the great planner that He is, He sent each of us here with at least one guardian angel. Also, we may have different angels that come in and out of our lives at different times to assist our guardian angel. Since the angels aren't limited to our concept of time and space, they can be with many people at the same time.

If life seems overwhelming to you, just imagine how a child feels. Introducing meditation techniques to a young child can become a lifelong gift. These meditations are a fun way to help our children relax, and in most cases to help them concentrate, whether at home or in a classroom. These meditations can be done lying down (my after-school students bring a pillow), sitting in a chair, or riding in a car. The main objective is for the child to feel comfortable and safe from within. The craft is a concrete visual that can help guide the child to that special journey or meditation at home. I have used these meditations many times with my first-grade class.

Roller-Coaster Breathing Exercise

(Parents, be sure to say all the meditations in a calm, soothing voice.)

All right, settle yourself down. Take in a big, deep breath. Hold it (for a count of two) … and now breathe out. As you take in another deep breath through your nose, picture yourself going up a roller coaster. As you breathe out through your nose, picture yourself going down the roller coaster. (Repeat two or three more times.) With your eyes closed, look straight ahead. You will begin to see a big, beautiful white ball of light. This ball is filled with love. As it comes closer, you can see that it has sparkles swirling around it. Keep breathing. Every time you breathe out, the white ball gets closer to you. With your next breath, imagine that you are breathing in the sparkles and white light. You can feel this peaceful light starting to enter at the top of your head; the sparkling light slowly travels down your body. It's in your head. Now it's around your shoulders and down your arms and into your fingers. It's traveling through your tummy, down your legs, and into your toes. Now you are relaxed! Here we go! (The Roller-Coaster Breathing Exercise should be done before every meditation.)

Meet Your Guardian Angel

Say to your child: *We were all born with at least one guardian angel. You will meet your guardian angel on many of these meditations. Remember, you can talk to your angel all the time. Make sure to call your angel by his or her name because they like that.*

Your guardian angel is your own special gift from God. Your angel's job is to guide and protect only you on this Earth, no one else. Isn't that great? Angels love to be kept busy. You can ask your angels to help you with all good things. Angels have one rule for you to remember – they can't help you with anything unless you ask them. So, talk to them often and don't forget to thank them!

- I refer to the guardian angel as "she" in this book. Please feel free to use "he" if your child's guardian angel is a male.

(First do the Roller-Coaster Breathing Exercise.)

You are walking through a beautiful field. There is green grass everywhere. Look from side to side, and enjoy all the beautiful flowers. The flowers are very colorful and seem to be everywhere! Keep walking. What else do you see? What do you hear? Pay close attention to everything around you. Do you smell anything? Do you see anyone or anything? As you walk, you see a little house up ahead. As you get closer to the house, you are getting very excited. You see a beautiful angel. You can't wait to meet your angel. When you finally reach the angel, you can say, "Hello."

This is your guardian angel. Your angel has been waiting to meet you! Your angel is so happy you have come to spend time with her. Pay very close attention to what she looks like. What is your angel wearing? Ask the angel for her name; listen carefully for an answer. Don't worry if your angel doesn't give a name right now; you have a lifetime to learn it. Does your angel have an animal? Sometimes your angel will appear with an animal that helps to protect you. Sometimes when you are scared, you can picture that animal right by your side. Do you have any questions for your angel? (Pause.) Is there anything you have always wanted to know? Are you worried about something or are you happy? Let your angel know. Your angel is here for you. As you two start walking toward the house, ask your angel if she has a message for you. Tell your angel that you will come back to visit again. Say good-bye. On the count of three, come back to me.

⏰ Sharing Time

Questions

- What does your guardian angel look like?
- What is her name? If the angel did not give a name, keep asking; the angel will reveal a name.
- Did your angel have a message for you?

🎨 Art Project 1: Guardian Angel Watercolor

What you will need:

- Watercolors and brushes
- Paper

Directions:

- Recreate the visit with your guardian angel through your own painting.

🎨 Art Project 2: Guardian Angel Pillowcase

What you will need:

- Standard pillowcase
- Fabric paints and brushes
- Lace or feathers (optional)

Directions:

- Have your child paint on his or her angel pillowcase. The pillow will help the child sleep well at night, during naptime, at camp, at Grandma's, and so on.

Magic Carpet Ride

(First do the Roller-Coaster Breathing Exercise.)

As you begin walking, you look up ahead and see something hovering. You run up to see what it is. As you get closer, you realize that it is a huge magic carpet! It's the biggest and most colorful carpet you have ever seen! It finally lands by your feet. It has come to take you for a ride. Climb aboard! Be careful; it can be wiggly. Zoooom! And you're off, headed straight for the sky! The carpet has big tassels on the corners. Every time your carpet takes a dip, a tassel flies up in the air. Your tummy flips every time the carpet twists and turns. Fun! You can feel the warmth from the sun on your shoulders as you dart around the white, fluffy clouds. If there is a special place you would like to visit, now is the time to ask the carpet to take you there. If not, just enjoy the wonderful places the carpet would like to share with you. Look down; what do you see? Are there buildings, people, or animals? Where are you? How do you know where you are? What do you see? Pay very close attention; you will visit magical places or different countries. You are so happy; you feel so free. Watch out! Hold on tight as you swoop around. It's time to bring the carpet in for a landing. On the count of three, come back to me.

⏰ Sharing Time

Questions:

- What did your magic carpet look like?
- Where did you go?
- What did you see?
- How did you feel?

🖼 Art Project: Magic Carpet

What you will need:

- A carpet square (alternative: square pillow or fabric placemat)
- Tempura or fabric paints and brushes
- Yarn for tassels

Directions:

- Have your child decorate his or her own magic carpet.
- The child can sit on the magic carpet anytime he or she wants to meditate!

Fairyland

(First do the Roller-Coaster Breathing Exercise.)

You are walking down a dirt road. It's warm and sunny. Everything looks so colorful and sparkly! As you look around, you notice many amazing trees. They are the most beautiful trees you have ever seen. Walk very slowly. If you look closely, you might see some movement around the trees. The fairies like to hide in the trees and bushes. All of a sudden, you see a big mushroom. It's the size of a basketball! Go over to it and get a closer look. You can't believe what you have just seen. All of a sudden, a little fairy flies out and says, "Hello!" Ask the fairy its name. What does the fairy look like? Ask the fairy to take you to Fairyland. The fairy tells you that she would love to take you to Fairyland, but on one condition: you cannot touch the fairies. You probably couldn't catch one if you tried. Fairies are very fast!

As you walk along with your fairy, you notice that the forest has come to an end. At the edge of the forest, you look down into a valley and see a wonderful little world. You have arrived at Fairyland! Notice how shiny and colorful everything is. Fairies love shiny things! Take gentle steps toward Fairyland. What do you see? Do you see fairy houses? They will be hidden in the trees! Be sure to check under the brightly colored mushrooms! Be sure to check around the lake or waterfall. Fairies are everywhere! Investigate very carefully. Fairies can be very hard to see. Tree fairies wear green and brown so they can blend in with the trees. Water fairies wear shades of blue and green to blend in with the water. Snow fairies wear white. Fairies are all around us in the outdoors. We just have to be really aware of them. Ask your fairy guide if she knows of anything the fairies would like you to know. Listen carefully. Your fairy tells you that if you want to find fairies in your own backyard, put some candy or coins out there. Don't forget that they love shiny things! On the count of three, come back to me.

⏱ Sharing Time

Questions:

- What does your fairy look like?
- What is your fairy's name?
- What does Fairyland look like?
- How many fairies did you see?
- Did your fairy have a message for you?

▨ Art Project: Fairy House

What you will need:

- A little wooden birdhouse
- Tempura paints and brushes
- Glitter
- Silk flowers and/or plastic gems

Directions:

- Paint the fairy house. Glue on flowers, gems, and glitter.
- Hang it in a tree, or place it somewhere outdoors for fairies to visit. Urge the child to meditate outdoors, near the fairy house.

Magical Telescope

(First do the Roller-Coaster Breathing Exercise.)

You are walking down a road, and you are very excited. You see your guardian angel waiting for you up ahead. As you approach, you see something very interesting in your angel's hand. When you finally meet her, your angel tells you that she is going to take you on a special, magical journey. Your angel thought it would be fun to explore with a magical telescope! She hands you the most beautiful telescope you have ever seen! As you hold the telescope, you are filled with excitement. Take the telescope with both hands, and gently examine it.

You are amazed at how magnificent the telescope is. It has brilliant colors and ribbons. What else does it have? Does it have any sparkly gems? Does it have any pictures on it? As you place the telescope up to your eye, magical things start happening! Your angel tells you to take her hand. Off you go! You start to float away—up, up, and away! You are floating among the clouds with your angel by your side! You feel as light as a feather. You are so happy. As you look through your magical telescope, you can't believe your eyes! You see the most beautiful colors and shapes. What do you see? Now you are over the ocean! Hold on! What a great time you are having! It's time to come in for a landing. Your angel tells you to keep your telescope in a safe place and to remember she is ready to travel at any time. On the count of three, come back to me.

🕐 Sharing Time

Questions:

- What did your telescope look like?
- Where did you go?
- What did you see?

🖼 Art Project: Magical Telescope

What you will need:

- An empty paper towel roll
- Tempura paints and brushes
- Glitter
- Ribbons

Directions:

- Paint the paper towel roll and then add ribbons and glitter. Urge your child to go outdoors and explore with his or her magical telescope.

5

Wishing Well

(First do the Roller-Coaster Breathing Exercise.)

You are walking through an enchanted forest, and you see your guardian angel. Your angel has been waiting for you. Today your angel is going to take you to a special waterfall. As you walk along, you can tell your guardian angel anything that is on your mind. Remember, your angel loves when you talk to her. Your angel points up ahead, where you spot a huge waterfall. It's the biggest waterfall you have ever seen. When you reach it, the cool water feels good against your skin as it sprays you. You can see little animals drinking from the water. It feels very peaceful. Even the animals seem to be happy. They are playing with each other.

What kinds of animals do you see? As you look around, you see something interesting. You ask what it is, and your angel brings you over to a beautiful wishing well. She explains that it is a magical wishing well. It is very round and tall. It is made of colorful blocks that keep changing colors. The roof is made of beautiful flowers. You can see birds sitting on the roof, and they are chirping a happy song. The rope that carries the pail is golden. The pail is rainbow colored. It's the most beautiful wishing well you have ever seen. Your angel hands you three colored stones. She says that you can make three wishes. Each time you make a wish, you can toss a colored stone into the well. As your wishes come true, you can use the stones for more wishes. Remember, your wishes can be used for other people, for animals, and for our entire world. Your angel reminds you that it is time to come back. You can always make wishes. On the count of three, come back to me.

⏲ Sharing Time

Questions:

- What did the forest look like?
- Describe the wishing well.
- What did the magic stones look like?
- Did you make three wishes?

🏛 Art Project: Wishing Well

What you will need:

- A plastic cup or a long, round container
- Craft paints and brushes
- Pipe cleaners
- "Magic" stones (colored stones found in the crafts or gardening section.)

Directions:

- Paint the container.
- When it dries, punch out two holes on opposite sides and tie a pipe cleaner to each side, creating a handle for the wishing well.
- Make wishes, and place the stones in the well. When a wish comes true, reuse the magic stone for another wish.

6

Cloud Connection

(First do the Roller-Coaster Breathing Exercise.)

It's a warm, bright, sunny day. You are walking barefoot in a big, beautiful field, surrounded by miles of green grass. You can feel the grass between your toes. It tickles. You can also smell the grass. It smells sweet, like lollipops. As you look around, you see colorful butterflies fluttering about along with birds swooping back and forth, singing and chirping. As you walk through the field, you can feel the sun on your shoulders. The warmth feels so good. You can't help looking up at the clouds. They seem especially lively today.

You begin to feel a little sleepy. You decide to lie down on your back and look up at the clouds. It feels nice to just lounge in the grass, put your hands behind your head, and relax. As you let your mind wander, you begin to notice that the clouds are turning into funny shapes. As you continue to look up, you can't believe your eyes! The clouds are playing tricks. What do you see? Maybe you begin to see funny animals floating across the sky. Maybe you see a ship floating by. Whatever you see, keep watching as a story begins to unfold. It's like watching a movie. Relax and enjoy the show. Where's the popcorn? On the count of three, come back to me.

🕐 **Sharing Time**

Questions:

- What did you see?
- What kinds of tricks did the clouds play?

🖼 **Art Project: A Blue Sky with Crazy Clouds**

What you will need:

- A piece of blue construction paper or white paper colored blue
- Cotton balls or loose cotton

Directions:

- Make shapes with the cotton on the blue paper.

7

Three, Two, One ... Blast Off!

(First do the Roller-Coaster Breathing Exercise.)

You are walking down a road. As you look around, you notice a shimmering object just up ahead. As you get closer, you can hardly believe your eyes! Standing right in front of you is the biggest and shiniest rocket ship you have ever seen! When you look up, the rocket ship looks like it is touching the clouds. Give the door a great big knock. Is anyone inside? You don't hear anything. Turn the knob to see if the rocket ship is unlocked. The handle turns, and you enter!

As you look around in the dark, all you see is a huge, flashing control panel. You take a seat in the big chair and can't believe how many buttons there are. As you start to explore all of these shiny buttons, you feel rumbling under your feet and almost fall out of your chair. Hold on tight! All of a sudden, you hear a loud voice that says, "Strap on your seatbelt, and get ready for takeoff. Ten, nine, eight, seven, six, five, for, three, two, one … blast off!" With a little jolt, you're off! The flashing lights are exciting to watch. You don't have to touch anything. The rocket ship has a mind of its own. It knows exactly what to do.

Look out the window. What do you see? As you approach outer space, you notice a very black sky with very bright stars all around. You're the captain of the ship! As you look around, you see many planets. Find an interesting planet to land on. As you land, the door pops open. You stick your head out and look around. You slowly climb down the ladder. What do you see? Have fun exploring! (Pause.) On the count of three, come back to me.

🕐 Sharing Time

Questions:

- What did the spaceship look like?
- What did you see?
- What did your planet look like?
- Did you see anything unusual?

🖼 Art Project: Outer Space Artwork

What you will need:

- A piece of large, black construction paper
- Space foam shapes from the craft store
- Star stickers

Directions:

- Create a piece of artwork by placing stars and foam shapes on the paper to recreate your trip to outer space!

8

Santa's Sleigh

(First do the Roller-Coaster Breathing Exercise.)

You are walking down a snowy road. Everywhere you look, you see lots and lots of white snow. It's snowing so hard that you begin to look like a snowman! You notice that the snow banks are taller than you. It's really beautiful. You notice that each sparkly snowflake looks amazing as it falls softly, gently joining with the other snowflakes, making beautiful patterns in the snow.

As you look ahead, you see something very shiny. You walk a little faster. As you get closer, you notice someone jumping up and down and waving his arms. Is it …? Do you think it could be …? You're right … it's Santa! He's been waiting for you! Santa welcomes you with a great big, "Ho, ho, ho" hug! Santa is so happy to see you. With a wink of his eye, he waves you over to show you a big, glistening object—his sleigh! It's the largest, reddest, shiniest sleigh you have ever seen!

Santa holds out his hand and helps you aboard. He tells you that he's going to take you for a test run on his sleigh before his Christmas flight! As soon as you get your seatbelt fastened, you're off. The reindeer are working together, steering the sleigh up, up, and away! Off you go! Hold on tight!

As you get comfortable, you notice all the flashing buttons on the dashboard. Santa explains that the sleigh is equipped with weather radar, a world map that lights up, and lots of other things. Santa asks you to assist him in making sure all his signals are working properly. Santa asks you if you have a license to drive the sleigh. Even though you don't have a license, Santa tells you that you can drive the sleigh … just for a minute. While you're driving, Santa is busy checking his lists of good boys and girls. He is also checking all the toys in his sack.

This is a special trip, so have lots of fun! Be sure to look down. What do you see? As the sleigh dips and turns, you can't believe your eyes! As you swoop around, you are able to see rooftops, cars, and lights in house windows. What do they look like? What do they remind you of? It's time to bring the sleigh in. As you unbuckle your seatbelt, Santa takes your hand to help you off the sleigh. He tells you that he will be visiting your home very soon. With a wink, he reminds you that he and the reindeer will probably be hungry. On the count of three, come back to me.

⏱ Sharing Time

Questions:

- What did the sleigh look like?
- Where did you go? How do you know?
- What did Santa say to you?

▧ Art Project: Santa's Sleigh

What you will need:

- An unpainted wooden sleigh from a craft store
- Craft or tempura paints and brushes
- Christmas foam pieces from a craft store

Directions:

- Paint Santa's sleigh from your memory. Remember, even though Santa's ride happens only once a year, you can meditate and talk to him every day!

9

Go Fly a Kite!

(First do the Roller-Coaster Breathing Exercise.)

You are walking through a grassy field. Everywhere you look, you see green grass. It smells as if it's just been cut. As you look around, you see lots of beautiful flowers that remind you of a rainbow. It's a warm, sunny day, but very windy. The sun feels good on your shoulders. You notice something flying around you. You place your hands around your eyes so you can look up. All of a sudden, a very colorful kite swoops down and lands at your feet! You pick it up with your hands, and before you know it, you're going up, up, and away! Hold on tight! The kite wants to take you on an adventure!

With every twist and turn, your tummy tickles! The kite sails right through the clouds and back down again! You realize just how lucky a kite's life really is. It can sail around the world and come back again. It can watch people in parks, animals on a farm, or play tag with the

clouds in the sky. Watch out, a bird just grabbed hold of the kite's tail. He's going along for the ride, too. You are sailing over a big park. You notice that there are many other kites in this park. You're coming in for a landing. Watch the treetops! As you let go, you notice that your family is waiting for you. They can't wait to hear where you have been. On the count of three, come back to me.

🕐 Sharing Time

Questions:

- What did your kite look like?
- How did it feel to fly through the air?
- Where did you go?

🖼 Art Project: A Kite

What you will need:

- A kite from the store
- Ribbons
- Fabric paints and brushes
- Bells (optional)

Directions:

- Take a kite, and paint it to make it your own. You can add some ribbons and bells and go flying any time!

10

The Magic Castle

(First do the Roller-Coaster Breathing Exercise.)

You are walking down a dirt road, and as you walk along, you notice a very tall building at the top of a very high mountain. The top of the mountain is surrounded by heart-shaped clouds. It looks very interesting, and you can't help but feel that another adventure awaits you if you can make it up the mountain. As you start up the mountain, you realize that the tall building is a castle! You run the rest of the way up.

As you approach the wooden door, you notice that it has a huge doorknocker on it in the shape of a crown. You pull down on the crown—bang, bang. All of a sudden, the door opens, and standing right in front of you is a beautiful princess. She is waiting for you. She tells you that she would love to show you all around the castle. "Let's go!" she says.

Every room is so special and unusual. Take a good look around. What do you see? The princess leads you into the large dining room and introduces you to the king and queen. They tell you to sit down. All of a sudden, cooks come out with trays and trays of food. They magically made all of your favorite foods! Dig in! Enjoy! As you finish your food, you begin to hear music. You look around and notice that the cooks have returned with beautiful cakes, cookies, and candies. As they dance through the door, they are singing, and the tootsie rolls are dancing on the trays. The princess tells you that you are very lucky. She tells you that the castle is a magical place. She explains that everything is not how it appears. The castle is full of magical tunnels and moving walls. She tells you that the only people allowed in the castle are children. You continue on your tour. Pay close attention, and have fun! On the count of three, come back to me.

⏰ Sharing Time

Questions:

- What did the castle look like?
- What did the princess look like?
- What did she say?
- What kind of magical things did you see in the castle?

🖼 Art Project: A Magical Castle

What you will need:

- Drawing paper (alternative: a wooden castle from a craft store)
- Princess stickers
- Tempura paints and brushes

Directions:

- Draw and/or paint the castle that you visited. Add stickers to create a really magical place.

11

The Lucky Leprechaun

(First do the Roller-Coaster Breathing Exercise.)

You are walking down a black road. As you look around, you see bright, colorful bushes. You notice lots of colorful flowers and four-leaf clovers everywhere! As you walk, you can't help but feel that this is a magical place. As you look around, taking in all that's around you, you feel a little tap on your shoulder. You turn quickly but don't see anything. You keep walking and feel another tap. This time you happen to look down. You can't believe your eyes! It is a leprechaun! He tells you that he is very excited to see you and that he has been waiting for you! He tells you that this is your lucky day. He has come to escort you to an enchanted forest where many leprechauns live. He explains that the leprechauns are very busy. It's a workday for them, and they are very busy making shoes. You must promise the leprechaun that you will just watch quietly and not disturb the other leprechauns. You agree. Off you go!

Your first stop is to a big, old tree that has a huge hole in the middle of it. The leprechaun tells you to look into the hole. When you do, you can't believe your eyes! You see some leprechauns hard at work. Some are nailing and gluing shoes. Some are stringing shoelaces in the finished shoes. Their little tools are really cute! Your leprechaun tells you that he wants to show you something very magical. He wants to take you to Leprechaun Park. It's a special park where leprechauns go with their families to relax.

As you approach the park, you hear lots of music. You jump down behind a bush and peek through. The leprechauns are dancing jigs and eating shamrock cookies. They are having a great time! All of a sudden, your leprechaun friend taps you on the shoulder and invites you to see something very colorful. Could it be … yes! It's a rainbow! As you stand under the rainbow, you can't believe how beautiful it is! You walk along and can see a pot of gold on the other side. The leprechaun tells you that you can look, but don't touch! He hands you a golden coin and tells you to keep it in your pocket for good luck. He says that if you ever get worried or sad, just rub the coin and good things will happen. On the count of three, come back to me.

🕐 Sharing Time

Questions:

- What did the leprechaun look like?
- What did he say?
- What did you experience in the enchanted forest?
- What would you do with all that gold?

🖼 Art Project: An Enchanted Leprechaun Village

What you will need:

- White, black, and yellow construction paper
- St. Patrick's Day stickers
- Paints and brushes or markers
- Gold glitter (optional)

Directions:

- Draw and color/paint an enchanted leprechaun village on the white paper.
- Use the black paper to make a pot.
- You can use the yellow paper to make gold coins.
- You can add glitter to make your village feel very enchanted.

Note: Around St. Patrick's Day, you can find a plastic pot and gold coins in craft stores. Your child can use the pot and coins throughout the year. (He or she can take adventures with the leprechauns all year!)

The Traveling Suitcase

(First do the Roller-Coaster Breathing Exercise.)

You are walking in a big field. Where are you? As you are about to take a step forward, you hear a loud grinding sound. As you whip your body around, you have to duck down quickly because a huge airplane flies right by you! Look out—here comes another! You find yourself at an airport. You managed to walk out onto the runway. As an airline worker puts the last suitcases on an airplane, he sees you and tells you that you must leave the runway immediately.

You turn and start to run back inside. As you look down, you spot something. When you finally reach the object, you see that it is a big box. You go over to the box to investigate. You get excited when you see it because you notice that the box has lots of colorful stickers and stamps on it. You move closer so you can see the writing on some of the stickers. You notice stamps from different countries! Is it ... yes, it's a suitcase that has traveled all around the world! Take your time and examine all the stamps and stickers. Now you decide to gently open the suitcase. As you touch the handle, though, you feel something strange. The suitcase starts shaking, and before you know it, you are flying around the world! Hold on tight; enjoy the ride! The suitcase can't wait to show you all the special places it has traveled. What country are you in? Don't forget to bring home souvenirs! On the count of three, come back to me.

⏱ Sharing Time

Questions:

- What did the suitcase look like?
- What kind of stickers and stamps did it have?
- Where did you travel with your suitcase?
- Did you bring back any souvenirs?

▦ Art Project: A Traveling Suitcase

What you will need:

- An unpainted wooden suitcase from a craft store
- Stickers and stamps of different places and countries from the scrapbooking section of a craft store (or cut out pictures from magazines)

Directions:

- Decorate your traveling suitcase with stickers and stamps.
- Place different items in the suitcase that have sentimental value to the child.

Unicorn Land

(First do the Roller-Coaster Breathing Exercise.)

You are walking in an enchanted forest. It is very beautiful. As you walk along, you can't help but notice how magical this forest seems. The sky is a bright blue, and the puffy clouds seem to dance around in the sky. This is a very busy place! You can hear the birds singing. Some of the animals are playing hide and seek. Up ahead, you see a beautiful lake with a waterfall. Over the waterfall is the most beautiful rainbow you have ever seen. You run over to get a good look at the graceful animals that are drinking from the lake. As you get closer, you realize that the animals are unicorns!

As you stare in amazement, you hear a soft voice say, "Welcome to Unicorn Land; we have been waiting for you." All of a sudden, the unicorns look at you and shake their heads up and down. Yes, they have all been waiting for you to arrive. They invite you to join them.

They ask if you would like to go swimming with them. You dip your foot into the water. The water is just right, so you jump in. The unicorns come over to you. You jump on one of the unicorns, and he gallops away. You feel like you're riding on a cloud! After your ride, you walk around, stroking the beautiful manes of all the unicorns. They smile and wink at you. How many do you see? Unicorns are God's magical creatures. They hold many secrets. They love to share information with you; all you have to do is talk to them. You can also share your secrets with them. Give it a try. They are great listeners! (Pause.) On the count of three, come back to me.

⏱ Sharing Time

Questions:

- What did the enchanted forest look like?
- How many unicorns did you see?
- What did the unicorns look like?
- Did they speak to you? What did they say?

▨ Art Project: Unicorns

What you will need:

- An unpainted wooden unicorn from the craft store
- Craft paints and brushes
- Glitter (optional)

Directions:

- Paint the wooden unicorn, and put glitter on its horn.

14

Fluttering Butterflies

(First do the Roller-Coaster Breathing Exercise.)

It is a warm and sunny day, and you are walking in a field of flowers. Take a deep breath and smell the wonderful flowers. They smell as sweet as candy! You are surprised that they seem to come in every shape and size. Some of the flowers are as tall as you! It looks like a rainbow burst, and all of the colors fell down and painted the flowers. The warm sun on your shoulders is making you sleepy. You stop for a moment and begin to look around for a perfect place to sit down and rest. You spot a beautiful lake nearby.

As you approach the lake, you see a little butterfly flutter past you. As you begin to look around, you see many butterflies—hundreds of butterflies. They seem to come in many shapes and sizes. They are as colorful as the flowers! You are fascinated as you watch them land on the flowers and fly away. They seem to be moving to music. As you start to chase some of them, they chase you back. You are having fun playing with them. They love to land on your shoulder. When you put your finger out, they come in for a landing! You finally make it to the lake. You lie on the grass beside the water and stretch your arms out behind your head. You love to sit and relax sometimes. The butterflies hover over the water. They are always on the move. They really don't stay in one place more than a few seconds. They are fun to watch. Just relax and enjoy their peacefulness. (Pause.) On the count of three, come back to me.

⊕ Sharing Time

Questions:

- What did the butterflies look like?
- How did you feel when you sat down to watch them?

▣ Art Project: A Butterfly Mobile

What you will need:

- Colorful construction paper
- Pipe cleaners
- A plastic hanger
- Tempura paints and brushes

Directions:

- Draw and cut out butterflies, and then paint them
- Add pipe cleaners for antennae, and use them to fasten the butterflies to the hanger to create a mobile. Scrunch the pipe cleaners to make the butterflies look as though they are flying.
- Hang the mobile in a child's room.

The Bunny Trail

(First do the Roller-Coaster Breathing Exercise.)

You are walking down a colorful brick path. As you look closely, you realize that they are not bricks at all! The path is made of jellybeans! The jellybeans look so yummy! You feel like you just want to scoop them up and shove them into your mouth! Keep walking, and make sure to notice everything around you. As you look forward, you see a very cute and colorful little house. It has many colorful Easter eggs in the front yard. You go over to the house and knock on the door. Who lives in this house, you wonder? Why, it's the Easter Bunny's house! He comes to the door with a great big, "Hello, there!" He invites you in.

The Easter Bunny was working hard, putting together Easter baskets just before you came. As you walk through the door, you can't believe your eyes! There are chocolate bunnies everywhere! There are all kinds of candy all over the place! The Easter Bunny has marshmallow chicks of all colors. He asks you if you would like to help him put the baskets together. You can't wait to help! After you are done, he tells you that it's time for him to take his daily walk down the bunny trail, and he wants to know if you would like to join him. Off you go!

You can't believe it! You are walking along a jellybean path with the Easter Bunny. His ears are so big and floppy that every time he takes a step with his big, fluffy feet, his ear taps you on the head. He introduces you to all of his friends. Bunny promises each one of his friends that they can expect a wonderful Easter basket on Easter morning.

As you walk along, the Easter Bunny tells you about some magic eggs that he makes. He can't wait to show them to you! As you're walking, you see something up ahead in the middle of a field. The field's grass is made of the grass you find in an Easter basket. The grass is made up of colors like green, purple, and pink! He takes you over to a huge chocolate basket in the middle of the field. He tells you to look in the basket. When you do, you can't believe your eyes! You see the most beautiful colored eggs! Bunny tells you to put your ear close to the eggs. "Listen carefully," he says. "They have a secret to share." (Pause.) On the count of three, come back to me.

⏱ Sharing Time

Questions:

- What did the Easter Bunny's house look like?
- What did he look like? What was he wearing?
- What did he say to you?
- What secret did the eggs have?
- What made them magical?

🖼 Art Project 1: Easter Bunny Artwork

What you will need:

- A large piece of construction paper
- Easter foam pieces
- Jellybeans
- Easter basket grass

Directions:

- Paste figures on the construction paper to recreate the scene at the Easter Bunny's house.

🖼 Art Project 2: Magic Easter Eggs

What you will need:

- Plastic Easter eggs from the store
- Craft paints and brushes

Directions:

- Paint and decorate the magical Easter eggs.

16

Boat Ride Ocean Side

(First do the Roller-Coaster Breathing Exercise.)

You are walking along a sandy beach. The warmth of the sun feels good on your shoulders. A gentle breeze kicks waves up against your legs. The cool water feels very refreshing against your skin. You breathe in the salt air and begin to relax. Off to the side, you see some seagulls squawking, as if they are trying to talk to you. In the distance, you hear a horn. As you look way out across the water, you see something. As you get closer, you see that it is a big boat coming toward you. Some people are waving at you. You begin to wave back. As soon as it comes ashore, the captain calls to you and invites you to come aboard and take a magical boat ride. You are very excited as you board the boat because you know another adventure awaits you.

As the boat sails away, the captain introduces you to the crew and some other people on the boat. They explain that you will all be going snorkeling in the ocean. Everyone is very excited. You are excited because you have never been able to explore at the bottom of the ocean. You wonder what you might find down there. You let your imagination run wild.

After a short boat ride, the crew drops anchor. They help you and the others with your snorkel gear and help you over the side of the boat. The crew leads you down into the ocean. The water is a crystal clear blue. As you start to explore, you can't believe your eyes! You see very odd yet very beautiful fish! They are the colors of the rainbow! They swim so fast that you can't catch them! You see coral in many different colors. The coral has little caves. You enter the coral to investigate. Oh my! The ocean is a very busy place! Look at all the starfish! (Pause.) On the count of three, come back to me!

⏱ Sharing Time

Questions:

- What did the boat and crew members look like?
- How did it feel when you were exploring underwater?
- What did you see?

▣ Art Project: Ocean in a Bowl

What you will need:

- A small, round glass bowl (like a fishbowl)
- Craft paints and brushes
- Regular or colored sand from a craft store
- Sea shells, starfish, etc.

Directions:

- Paint the glass bowl with ocean items.
- Place sand at the bottom of the bowl.
- Add seashells, starfish, etc., to the bottom of the bowl.

The ocean in a bowl makes a good visual for meditation. It brings you right back to the ocean.

17

Magic Slippers

(First do the Roller-Coaster Breathing Exercise.)

You are walking barefoot down a road when all of a sudden you look down and can't believe your eyes! A pair of slippers has magically appeared on your feet! They are the most beautiful slippers you have ever seen. They fit perfectly. You feel like you are walking on clouds! Before you can even blink, the slippers have you running, skipping, and jumping down the road. The slippers are going to take you on another adventure! Wow!

Suddenly, you find yourself dancing on a stage in Ireland, performing an Irish step dance. There are many other children performing with you, and they have on their magic slippers too. You can't believe how all the slippers are dancing together. It is truly magical! When the show is over, as soon as you take a bow, you're off! You now find yourself on a big stage in New York City. You are performing in a big musical show. It's so much fun! When the final curtain comes down, you are off again! Next you find yourself skipping down a path in a park. The park is so quiet, with big, beautiful trees and green, green grass all around. There is a big fountain in the middle of the park. As you walk over to it, you see lots of birds, butterflies, flowers, and bunnies. It's a very peaceful place. You sit for a minute to rest.

All that dancing has left you a little tired. You close your eyes and listen to the water spraying out of the fountain. The sound of the water is relaxing; you start to daydream. You're not there very long when your slippers pick you up and start moving again. This time you find yourself at home, getting ready for bed. You carefully place your magic slippers beside your bed, knowing that they will be ready for your next adventure. (Pause.) On the count of three, come back to me.

⏱ Sharing Time

Questions:

- What did your slippers look like?
- Where did your slippers take you?
- What kinds of fun things did you see?

▣ Art Project: A Pair of Magic Slippers

What you will need:

- Colored construction paper
- Tempura paints and brushes
- Yarn or ribbon
- Glitter (optional)

Directions:

- Trace the child's feet on the construction paper and cut out.
- Paint the slippers.
- Tie the pair of slippers together with yarn or ribbon.

The child can hang the magic slippers in his or her bedroom and can go on adventures or meditations "by foot" any time.

18

All Aboard!

(First do the Roller-Coaster Breathing Exercise.)

You find yourself at a train station. You're standing on the platform waiting patiently for a train to arrive. It is very quiet. All of a sudden, you hear a thunderous roar! As you look down the track, you see a huge light barreling toward you. It's the train! You are very excited. As it comes to a screeching stop, the conductor yells out, "All aboard!" He is pointing to you! Get going, the train has come to take you on another adventure! As soon as you climb aboard, you feel a jolt, and then you hear the loud train whistle.

The train starts chugging away. You're sitting in your seat, waiting patiently for your adventure to begin, when the brakeman comes to get your ticket. You start searching for your ticket, carefully checking every pocket. Nothing. Your heart begins to beat quickly. What is going to happen? You have lost your ticket. The brakeman shakes his head and walks away. After a few minutes, he comes up to you and tells you that the conductor would like to see you. You go rushing through the cars to get to the conductor. You must explain why you don't have a ticket. He should understand.

The conductor silently stares as you tell him that you have lost your ticket. He doesn't move for a long while and then smiles and asks you if you would like to be the co-conductor! Oh yeah! No time to waste! You're coming to the next stop. You blow the whistle and pull on the brake with all your might. The train comes to a screeching halt. People are running back and forth. You yell, "All aboard!" And you're off! As the train goes rumbling through towns and farmlands, you get to see so many things up close. Look at all the cows! What else do you see? You tell the conductor that you must be getting home. When you arrive at your station, you begin to climb off the train. The conductor taps your shoulder, and as you turn around, you notice that he is holding a big golden ticket that says, "Passenger may ride this train anytime." You thank the conductor and tell him that you look forward to your next adventure with him. On the count of three, come back to me.

⏲ Sharing Time

Questions:

- What did the train look like?
- What did it feel like to be co-conductor?
- Where did you take the train?
- What did you see on the way?

🎨 Art Project: My Train

What you will need:

- An unfinished wooden train car(s) from the craft store
- Craft paints and brushes
- Paper

Directions:

- Paint the train car(s) as you saw it/them on your adventure.
- Draw a train ticket you can use on future train adventures.

19

The Dream Box

(First do the Roller-Coaster Breathing Exercise.)

You are walking through a beautiful garden where there are lots of sweet-smelling flowers and fluttering butterflies. You love visiting this garden. It is very peaceful and relaxing here. You find your favorite big rock to sit on. Up ahead you see your guardian angel. She starts waving to you as she comes toward you. She has been waiting for you. You are so glad to see her and give her a big hug. You can't help but notice that she has a very beautiful object in her hand.

You ask about the object your angel is holding. She tells you that she has brought you a very special present. She calls it a dream box. The box is painted in your favorite colors. You carefully open it up and examine it. It is empty. You ask your angel why it is empty and what the beautiful box is used for. She says it is empty because she wants you to put things in the box that you dream about. She says to write all of your dreams or wishes on pieces of paper and place the papers in your box. She says that you don't have to worry about how your dreams will come true. She tells you to leave the "how" part to God. You should just do the dreaming.

Your angel tells you that everything is made up of energy, even words. She tells you that when you say something or write something down, it carries lots of energy. She says that when a dream or wish comes true, you may throw that piece of paper away. Your box can always be filled with dreams and wishes. That's what life is made of. You may also place dreams or wishes you have for others—your family, your friends, or others in the world. God loves when we think of others. The two of you walk a little more. You share some of your dreams with her. It's time to be getting back. Tell your angel that you will see her again soon. On the count of three, come back to me.

🕐 Sharing Time

Questions:

- What did the dream box look like?
- What kinds of dreams do you have?

🎨 Art Project: A Dream Box

What you will need:

- An unfinished wooden box from a craft store
- Craft paints and brushes
- Foam objects, gems, glitter (optional)

Directions:

- Paint the wooden box.
- Decorate it with gems, glitter, or your favorite foam objects.
- Write your dreams or wishes on paper and place them in your dream box. Watch your dreams come true!

20

Talkin' Dolphin

(First do the Roller-Coaster Breathing Exercise.)

You're walking along a beach. The sand feels warm between your toes as you keep walking. Every time you breathe in, you can smell the ocean. With each whiff, you imagine all the sea animals that live and play in the ocean. As you're picturing sea lions, penguins, fish, clams, and whales, you hear a squeaking noise from the ocean. As you look out into the water, you spot a group of dolphins jumping and twisting their bodies. They seem to be having a great time! They seem to be dancing to a rock and roll song! They are having so much fun that you start to whistle, hoping one of the dolphins will hear you and come over.

As the dolphins continue to play around, one dolphin seems to be listening to the whistle. With a big splash, he dashes over to you. With his eyes, he seems to be telling you to grab a hold of his fin. You grab on, and you're off! You find yourself playing in the middle of the dolphins! They are very gentle and playful. You are having a great time! You jump on a dolphin's back, and he takes you down into the ocean. You see all kinds of colorful fish. You see beautiful coral and starfish.

It is time to come back to the surface. The dolphins are waiting for you to play ball with them. They are playing dolphin volleyball. They jump and hit the ball with their long noses. Did you know that dolphins are considered very close friends of the angels? They are known for bringing your worries to the angels. If you have any worries or concerns, you can always come back to talk and play with the dolphins! As you come ashore, you look back and see the dolphins give you a big wink and a wave. They'll be back! On the count of three, come back to me.

⏰ Sharing Time

Questions:

- How did it feel to swim and play with the dolphins?
- Where did you go, and what did you do?
- How many dolphins did you see?
- What did they say?

🖼 Art Project: Dolphin Artwork

What you will need:

- Construction paper
- Watercolor paints and brushes
- Dolphin foam pieces

Directions:

- Paint the ocean scene with the dolphins. You can add foam pieces and show the dolphins playing in the ocean. (Don't forget to include yourself in the scene!)

The Amazing Spectacles

(First do the Roller-Coaster Breathing Exercise.)

You are walking down a road. As you look ahead, you see a cute little monkey. He asks you if you have ever been to a jungle. You tell him no. He invites you to join him on a jungle adventure. He tells you that in order to have the best jungle adventure of your life, you must put on a pair of magical glasses. He hands you a funny pair of glasses. They are the silliest glasses you have ever seen. You put them on, and you're off!

You follow the monkey and climb right up a tree! He holds out a vine and tells you to swing across with him to another tree. One ... two ... three ... jump! What fun! Oh my goodness! You have grown a tail! You start swinging upside down from a branch. The jungle looks very funny upside down! You spot some bananas and have to jump over some very strange animals to get to them. Before you know it, some of the other animals are chasing after you. You have started a game called Capture the Banana. Everyone wants to play. It's their favorite jungle game. As you run by, you toss the bananas to a bird. He takes off with the bananas and passes them off to an armadillo. The armadillo passes the bananas to the giraffe, and he passes them on to the hippo. You are all having a great time. Along comes a big black bear, who is getting very hungry. He suggests that you light a fire and barbeque the bananas. Great idea! Grilled bananas, anyone? All the animals come to dinner. They love your magical glasses. They remind you to keep your glasses in a safe place and put them on whenever you are ready to meet up with them for a jungle adventure! (Pause.) On the count of three, come back to me.

⊕ Sharing Time

Questions:

- What did your magical glasses look like?
- What did it feel like to climb and swing as a monkey?
- What other animals did you see?
- How did you get to the bananas?

▦ Art Project: Magical Glasses

What you will need:

- A child's pair of plastic sunglasses (or large clown glasses)
- Foam pieces, gems, etc.
- Glue

Directions:

- Glue decorations on the sunglasses.

On the Wings of a Dove

(First do the Roller-Coaster Breathing Exercise.)

It's a warm, sunny day. You find yourself lying on the grass and watching the clouds go by. All of a sudden, you hear a sweet chirping song. You look over and see a white dove sitting on the edge of a water fountain. She winks at you. You can hardly believe your eyes! She flies over to you, and you notice that she has a long branch hanging from her beak. She motions for you to grab the branch. As soon as you do, you're off once again!

The dove explains that she is a symbol of peace around the world. She decides to take you around the world so you can see how other children live. As you look down, you realize you are flying above Japan. A group of children are waving to you calling, *"Kon'nichiwa."* They are swinging and want you to join them. You shout, "Hello" and zoom by. Before you know it, you find yourself in France. You ask the dove to swoop down so you can get a closer look. The children seem to be playing a game of tag. The children start to chase after you. They yell, "*Bonjour!*" Up you go, speeding through the air. Next stop, Israel. The children are playing ball at a playground. They wave to you and say, "*Shalom!*" You wave at the children as you zoom by. They wave their arms and shout for you to come back to play, but you are too busy flying to your next destination. You have arrived in Italy. You see some children fishing at the coast. They look up and wave as you go by. They shout, "*Ciao!*" You head for Spain, and the children shout, "*Hola,*" as they dance around in the street. "Come join us!" they shout.

The dove is getting a little tired and begins the journey back to the park. She tells you to remember that children around the world may look different, sound different, and dress differently. Then she says, "Remember, children also have many things in common. All children love to play, sing, and dance, and most of all, they love to live in peace. They especially enjoy hugs and kisses from family. People may look different on the outside, but we are all the same on the inside." The dove tells you that she needs your help to spread peace in the world. She asks you to help her by being kind to all children you might meet. Remember, they are really not much different than you.

🕐 **Sharing Time**

Questions:

- What did the dove look like?
- What did she tell you?
- What was your favorite country? Why?

🖼 Art Project: Multi-Cultural Peace Flag

What you will need:

- A piece of white cotton fabric
- Fabric markers
- Wooden stick for flagpole (optional)

Directions:

- Draw a big peace sign in the middle of the fabric. Write the names of different countries and their words for peace. (See below.)

Peace Around the World

Japan: *heiwa*

China: *heping*

France: *la paix*

Israel: *shalom*

Spain: *paz*

Germany: *der Frieden*

Italy: *pace*

Russia: *mir*

Note: Did you know that the peace sign is said to be a dove's footprint upside down? The flag will remind you of the peace dove and her message for peace around the world.

I hope your children love these meditations as much as my students did. I would love to hear about their magical journeys. If you would like to share the children's adventures with me, contact me at my website, magicaljourneykids.com.

lisa@magicaljourneykids.com